Ethiopian Kitchen
YOU CAN MAKE INJERA

Ethiopian Bridges Publishing
Proceeds benefit Clinic at a Time Inc.

ETHIOPIAN KITCHEN
YOU CAN MAKE INJERA

Recipe development: Mulusew Yayehyirad
Content, editing and design: Teresa Peneguy Paprock
Original photography: John-Brian Paprock

© 2011, Ethiopian Bridges Publishing: All rights reserved. No part of this publication may be reproduced or distributed in any form or by any means, or stored in a database or retrieval system, without the prior written permission of the publisher. Requests to the publisher should be addressed to Ethiopian Bridges Publishing, c/o Clinic at a Time Inc., PO Box 14457, Madison, WI 53708.

Limit of Liability/Disclaimer of Warranty: While the publisher and author have used their best efforts in preparing this book and website, they make no representations or warranties with respect to the accuracy or completeness of the contents of this book and website and specifically disclaim any implied warranties of merchantability or fitness for a particular purpose.

ISBN 978-1-4583-5643-7

This book is dedicated to my dear mother, W/RO Etayehu Demisse. It is because of her that I became the kind of person I am today. She was gentle, loving, caring and such a kind human being. She taught me to be kind, loving and caring just like her.

One of her responsibilities as a mother was to teach me how to be a good cook. Among her great qualities, cooking was one of them. She was known to be one of the most gifted cooks (balemuya) in the area where we lived. When I founded Clinic at a Time, she was one of the driving forces; she gave me tireless support, from sharing ideas to helping me with my children, to cooking for hours for our fundraising events.

I will miss her spiritual, motherly and friendly presence. I am so thankful to her for raising me with great values, to put God's will before my own personal needs and to think about others.

*– Mulusew Yayehyirad
executive director, Clinic at a Time Inc.*

CONTENTS

Grocery list 7

Introducing Ethiopia.. 9

Introducing Ethiopian cuisine.................................13

Introducing injera..15

Making injera...17

Making tibs (beef dish) 34

Making yekik alicha (split-pea dish)........................38

Making gomen (mixed greens dish).........................42

Enjoying a traditional Ethiopian dinner..................47

About Clinic at a Time Inc. 50

Acknowledgements 53

GROCERY LIST
To make the dishes in this book, you will need:

COOKING ITEMS, CONDIMENTS
Barley flour
Canola oil
Garlic, minced
Ginger root, minced
Olive oil
Rosemary, fresh
Salt
Teff flour*
Turmeric
Whole wheat flour
Yeast, dry

MEAT
Boneless top sirloin steak

VEGETABLES
Collard greens, chopped, frozen
Jalapeño peppers
Spinach, chopped, frozen
Tomatoes
Turnip greens, chopped, frozen
Yellow onions
Yellow split peas, dried

APPLIANCES, UTENSILS
Cooking pan for injera**
Deep pan
Measuring cup
Sefed *(see page 31)*
Tablespoon
Teaspoon
Tight-seal storage containers
Wooden spoon

OPTIONAL
Red wine, berbere spice *(for tibs)*

* See next page for ordering teff flour. Although teff flour is traditionally used to make injera, other flours can also be used including millet, wheat, rice, barley or corn.

**See next page for ordering a free-standing injera pan. Information about using a frying pan on the stove is on page 31.

WHERE TO FIND TEFF FLOUR

You will need equal parts of ivory teff flour and brown teff flour. We recommend ordering teff flour from The Teff Company, an Idaho-based supplier of American-grown Mascal Teff for nearly 20 years. The Teff Company's teff is available at some natural food stores, and also by mail order. Information is available at www.teffco.com (info@teffco.com) or by calling toll-free, (888) 822-2221. Ask for the brown teff to be double-ground.

WHERE TO FIND AN INJERA PAN

It is important to have a pan dedicated only to injera, whether it  is a frying pan for the stove or a free-standing pan. If you choose to purchase a free-standing pan, we recommend the 16-inch 735 Silverstone Teflon-coated Heritage Grill with premium non-stock finish, from Bethany Housewares Inc. *(Do not use aluminum.)* The grill, often referred to as a lefse grill, is available at a number of national outlets including Target and Amazon. However, the lid does not come with the pan; to order a lid, you can contact Bethany directly at (563) 547-5873 or sales@bethanyhousewares.com, or ask your local retailer to order a lid for you.

INTRODUCING ETHIOPIA

"The origin of Ethiopia is largely the origin of us all." – Javier Gozalbez

Tucked inside the Horn of Africa lies the country of Ethiopia, a place as stunning in its natural beauty as it is rich in culture and history.

Bordering Somalia, Kenya, Eritrea and the Sudan, Ethiopia is considered by many to be the very cradle of humankind: scientific evidence, including DNA research, suggests that the area was home to the earliest humans.

The skeleton of "Lucy," an Australopithecus afarensis of the Hominid species, was discovered in the Hadar region of Ethiopia in 1974; the species is believed to have lived in the area about 4 million years ago – and perhaps even earlier. Fragments of more than 300 other individuals of the species have been discovered in the region.

Ethiopia is one of the oldest countries in the world, and the oldest independent country in Sub-Saharan Africa. The Queen of Sheba is said to have visited King Solomon in 1000 BC. The King James

Version of the Bible contains the word "Ethiopia" 45 times. The wife of Moses is said to have been Ethiopian. And St. Philip baptized the first person into the Christian faith – an Ethiopian eunuch – in the Gazan desert there.

About twice the size of the state of Texas, the land of Ethiopia is geographically diverse, with lakes and rivers, savannahs and mountains, and lush forests. The Ministry of Culture and Tourism says Ethiopia has "13 Months of Sunshine," due to its mild climate. The country has 24 major wildlife preserves as well as a variety of rare indigenous animals including the kudu, the caracal, the galada baboon, and the oryx.

The 10th largest country on the African continent, Ethiopia is Africa's third most populous country, with a population of 82,825,000. The Ethiopians are a diverse people. More than 70 languages are spoken there, with Semitic, Nilo-Saharan, Cushitic and Omotic tongues represented. Amharic is the official language of Ethiopia, and is historically and linguistically one of the most important languages in the world.

Ethiopia is home to a wide spectrum of religious traditions. Statistical estimates vary dramatically according to the way the data is collected, but the two majority religions are Ethiopian Orthodox Christianity and Islam.

Orthodox Christianity was established in Ethiopia (then Abyssinia) as early as the Fourth Century. The Ethiopian Orthodox Church is noteworthy in that its Bible contains several unique books, and that it shares some practices with Conservative Judaism. The Church of Our Lady Mary of Zion, in Tigray Province, is said to possess the Ark of the Covenant that Moses carried during the Exodus.

Muslims immigrated from Mecca in the Seventh Century; Mohammed himself is said to have sent his followers there. Harar, in Eastern Ethiopia, is considered "The Fourth Holy City of Islam," with 82 mosques. Many Ethiopian Muslims follow the Sufi tradition.

A small but significant number of Ethiopians practice Judaism, mostly in the northern province of Gondar. Other minority religions in Ethiopia include Catholicism; a variety of sects of Protestantism; and Animism, a belief that souls exist not only in humans but also in animals and plants and in non-living entities such as rocks and thunderstorms.

About 3.4 million people live in the capital city of Addis Ababa, a bustling urban habitat that is the seat of government and education. Founded in 1886, the city is so important to the continent today – due to its historical, diplomatic and political significance – it's known as "The Political Capital of Africa." In the city, some 230,000 people work in the fields of trade, commerce, manufacturing and industry. Addis Ababa is home to a variety of museums, libraries, colleges, government buildings and shopping areas.

The city is surrounded by thousands of square miles dotted by small towns and villages, the majority of which are supported by agriculture.

Ethiopia's major exports include livestock, textiles, hides and skins, oil seeds and pulses, and – most notably – coffee. Ethiopia is proudly the birthplace of coffee, which derives its name from the Kaffa province of Ethiopia, and generates 60 percent of the country's total export earnings.

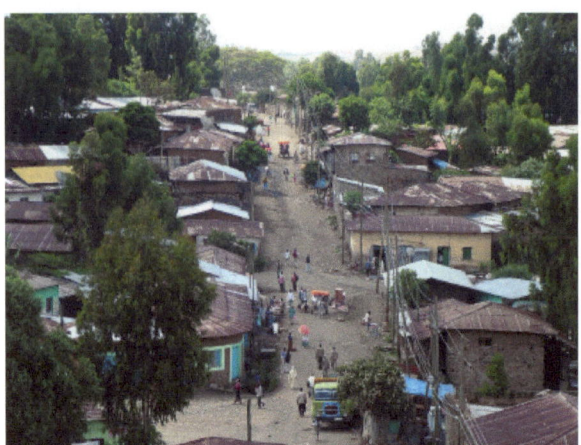

Considered by many to be the finest in the world, Ethiopia's coffee is uniquely smooth and savored for its high acidity and rich, full body. Coffee is not simply a beverage in Ethiopia; it's part of tradition. An elaborate coffee ceremony is an integral part of the cultural and social life in Ethiopia, and a visitor invited to the ceremony considers it an honor.

INTRODUCING ETHIOPIAN CUISINE

The cuisine of Ethiopia, and the traditional ways of enjoying it, is unique in all the world.

The food of Ethiopia (and that of neighboring Eritrea) is often hot and spicy – in a completely different way than, say, that of Mexico or Jamaica or India. Not all Ethiopian dishes are spicy (those selected for this book are mild). But eating a hot Ethiopian dish is a memorable experience.

Many spicy dishes from the region feature berbere (a mixture of fenugreek and red pepper along with cloves, ginger, chili peppers, coriander, rue berries, allspice, turmeric, cumin, and ajwain, toasted together). Berbere is sometimes made as a dry spice mix (it is available in Ethiopian stores, as well as online), and is sometimes made with oil or water to form a paste. Also adding to the spiciness of Ethiopian food is the use of onions and garlic, more familiar to the American palate.

Whether spicy or mild, Ethiopian cuisine offers vegetarian and meat dishes. The large percentage of Ethiopians that belong to the Ethiopian Orthodox faith observe 250 fasting days each year – which means more than half the time, adherents consume no meat, eggs or dairy. The extensive fasting has made it necessary for the Ethiopians to create a number of dishes that are vegan.

The most common dish Ethiopians serve is wot, a spicy stew featuring berbere. If vegetarian, it's made from chickpeas, potatoes or lentils; if it's a non-fasting day, wot can be made from beef, goat, fish, chicken, or lamb. (Pork is not served, as neither Ethiopian Orthodox Christians nor Muslims may eat it.) Doro wot (the chicken variety) is often served with hard boiled eggs.

Another option for non-fasting days is tibs, which is sautéed meat with onions and peppers. And those who enjoy raw meats would appreciate kitfo, which is marinated in chili powder and spiced butter. Ayib, a soft white Ethiopian cheese, is often simulated with cottage cheese in America, but ayib is deliciously distinct.

Beverages include tej, a potent wine made of honey and similar to mead, and tella, a home-brewed beer.

The Ethiopians say, "Those who eat from the same plate will not betray each other." The traditional Ethiopian meal is served to a group of people from a single, large plate, and is eaten by hand, without utensils.

If you are a guest, don't be surprised if your neighbor reaches out a hand to feed you. This is known as gursha, a uniquely Ethiopian – and honoring – custom. Ethiopians often hand-feed their guests. If this happens to you, realize that it is an action of respect and bonding; if you're comfortable doing so, you can return the favor.

The delectable morsel of food you are being offered will be wrapped in perhaps the most unique food of all – injera.

INTRODUCING INJERA

Injera is the traditional flatbread of both Ethiopia and Eritrea, and it is impossible to imagine the area's cuisine without it. A type of fermented flatbread, injera has a spongy texture and a slightly sour flavor.

Similar to a pancake or a crepe – but with more "eyes" on the top surface – injera serves as not only the "dish" (the food to eat) but the "dish" as well (the thing the food is on). A variety of stews and sauces are placed on the injera, which soaks up the juices and is used to scoop up the foods.

The staple of Ethiopia and Eritrea, injera is eaten every day, with most meals, in virtually every home in the region. It can be eaten with wot and tibs, or alone. It is served flat and rolled up. It is shredded and spiced for breakfast, and it holds dinner together.

Injera is a nutritious option when it comes to breads. Made traditionally, it has no gluten, and contains fiber, protein, iron and calcium.

The magical ingredient in injera – the thing that makes it so unique – is teff. Teff is a millet-like cereal grain that is indigenous to Ethiopia. Teff plays a major role in the economy of Ethiopia, and is starting to appear in some health stores in the United States. Its flavor is sweet and molasses-like.

The cook of the household in Ethiopia dedicates a considerable amount of time each week to the making of injera, with a process that rotates every three days. Americans who want to make injera face apparent obstacles – teff can be hard to find, and the steps for making it can seem complex.

But you can make injera. And we will show you how.

MAKING INJERA

Making injera, especially the first time, takes some planning ahead. And it can take practice to achieve the right consistency and taste. It's a good idea to read through all the instructions before you begin. The calendar below shows the timing of the three steps involved, assuming you plan to make injera on Saturday evening.

Ingredients for injera batter:

1 tsp. dry yeast
2 cups teff flour (use a mix of ivory and brown, equal parts. If you can only use one kind, use ivory)
2 cups barley flour
1 cup whole wheat flour*
3 cups warm water

*Wheat flour can be replaced by rice or corn flour, but it must be finely ground. If you use corn flour, do not use the type that's used to make cornbread.

SUN	MON	TUE	WED	THR	FRI	SAT
				Morning: STEP 1 Make batter		**Morning:** STEP 2 Add hot water **Evening:** STEP 3 Make injera

17

STEP ONE – 36-48 hours before you make the injera:

In a small container or cup, mix the dry yeast with ½ cup of water. Cover the container and let the mixture rise for 10-15 minutes. The purpose of this step is to dissolve and activate the yeast.

Now use a large container with a lid that seals tightly – such as a Tupperware. Mix the dissolved yeast with the teff, barley and whole wheat flour, slowly adding the 2½ remaining cups of water. This process is best done by hand. Knead the mix thoroughly until all the lumps are out and it feels very smooth.

After everything is mixed, cover the injera batter with the tightly-sealed cover and let it ferment at room temperature for 36-48 hours.

STEP TWO – 6-8 hours before making the injera:

Boil 2½ cups of water. Slowly add the hot water to the injera batter, using a long-handled spoon. Mix the batter with the water very well, using your hand to make sure that the mix that has settled at the bottom is well-mixed. Wait 6-8 hours.

STEP THREE – 6-8 hours later, it's time to make injera!

Set aside 1½ cups of injera batter to use as a starter for your next batch of injera. This starter is already fermented and needs to be refrigerated. When you make injera again (and we know you will!), follow the directions on page 20.

MAKING INJERA WITH YOUR OWN STARTER

When you make injera with your own starter, follow the process described in STEPS ONE, TWO AND THREE but with one exception: eliminate the dry yeast in STEP ONE and use the starter in its place.

You can keep the starter fresh for up to three months. Take it out of the refrigerator every two weeks, pour out the extra liquid that has settled on the starter (it will look dark), and add a cup of cold, fresh water. Mix it and put it back in the refrigerator.

When you are ready to use the starter, pour off the excess water. Let it sit at room temperature for 2-3 hours. If needed, add enough fresh water to make your starter the consistency of pancake batter. Now you are ready to make your batter.

Use a non-stick flat pan to make the injera. You can use a free-standing pan. Alternatively, you can use a shallow, non-stick frying pan on the stove (directions for making injera on the stovetop follow this section).

Dedicate a pan to be used only for injera. If you are using a pan that has been used for other things, your injera may stick to the pan or you will not have the pretty bubbly "eyes" on your injera. Never use oil, butter, or utensils on the pan.

To "cure" a brand-new pan and prevent injera from sticking, cover the bottom with salt, and heat it until hot. Then rub the salt in with a paper towel. You can cure the pan anytime before you make the injera - during the 6-8 hours you are waiting (between steps 2 and 3) is a good time. The more you use the pan, the easier it will become to remove the injera.

Heat the free-standing pan to 500 degrees. Using a cup with a spout, such as a measuring cup, pour the batter clockwise in a spiral fashion around the pan, from the outer edge to the center.

23

Cover the pan, as injera is cooked with the steam effect, not just the heat.

It takes only 20-45 seconds for a piece of injera to be ready. When you remove the lid, you will be able to tell the injera is ready because it will have bubbly "eyes."

Traditionally, a sefed – a round piece of wicker – is used to lift the injera off the pan. You can use a rimless, round cookie sheet or the cardboard circle from a frozen pizza. Or you can cut one yourself from a piece of cardboard. Do not use a spatula or any other utensil. Make sure the tool you use to remove the injera does not scrape your pan.

The edge of the injera will be a bit crusty, curling up. Lift one side of the injera with one hand, and use the other hand to slide your sefed underneath. Then simultaneously lift and pull the injera gently off the pan.

Let it cool on the sefed while you are preparing the next piece of injera. As each is made, pile the cooked injera on a plate or tray. If they have cooled, they will not stick to each other.

Hint: If for some reason your batter is a bit thick and makes your injera "fat," just keep going; do not add additional water. If you add extra water to the fermented mix, your injera will not turn out well.

When it's time to clean the pan, simply rub it with a paper towel and some salt. Any residue can be cleaned off this way. Do not use water and dish soap to clean the pan.

This recipe makes 6-10 pieces of injera, depending on the size of pan you are using. If you want to make more injera, double or triple the recipe. Injera can be refrigerated or frozen for storage. One option is to cut it into fourths, which will easily fit in a gallon Ziploc storage bag. You can store injera in your freezer for up to 6 months.

Cooking injera with a shallow frying pan on the stove:

Use a shallow frying pan not less than 12 inches across. The best option is a Teflon, non-stick pan. The pan must be dedicated to cooking only injera. See page 21 for the proper way to care for the pan, and for instructions on how to "cure" a new pan.

Heat the pan to medium-low on the stove. Pour the batter into the pan as if you were making a pancake. You can tilt the pan to make sure the batter covers the bottom evenly. Cover the pan with a lid during cooking. When you are finished cooking the injera, clean the pan by rubbing it using a paper towel and salt.

CONGRATULATIONS! You have made injera!

Following are three recipes – a meat dish, a pea dish and a greens dish – that will help you create an Ethiopian meal for four. These are mild dishes (although you can add berbere to spice up the meat dish) and quite easy to make.

TIBS (BEEF DISH)

2 lbs. boneless top sirloin steak, cubed
2 yellow onions, medium (cut julienne style – into long thin strips)
1 Roma tomato, medium
4 Tbsp. olive oil
1 jalapeño pepper (seeded and cut julienne style)
1 pinch salt
2 Tbsp. berbere spice (optional)
1 Tbsp. fresh rosemary, chopped
1 cup red wine (optional)

Warm your pan. Don't add the oil yet!

Brown the meat on medium-high.

When the meat is medium rare, add onion and tomato. Then add the olive oil.

Add the jalapeño pepper, salt and fresh rosemary. (Optional: Add berbere spice and one cup red wine. Simmer for another 3-5 minutes for juicier tibs.) Cook through and remove from heat.

YEKIK ALICHA (SPLIT PEA DISH)

1 cup yellow split peas (dried)
2½ cups water
2 yellow onions, medium (chopped)
4 Tbsp. canola oil
1 pinch salt
½ tsp. turmeric for color
1 jalapeño pepper (seeded and cut julienne style – into long thin strips)
1 Tbsp. minced garlic
1 Tbsp. minced ginger root
½ cup water

In a 4-5 cup-sized saucepan, mix the first two ingredients. Cook the peas on medium-high heat on the stovetop for 30 minutes or until soft, stirring occasionally.

In another pan, sauté the onion and the oil. Cook until onions are soft and translucent.

Add the cooked peas, pinch of salt, turmeric, and minced garlic and minced ginger in to the pan. Continue stirring occasionally.

Add the remaining half-cup of water. Stir all ingredients together, turn the heat to low and cook the water down for 10 more minutes, stirring occasionally.

Finally, add the jalapeño pepper and remove from heat.

GOMEN (MIXED GREEN DISH)

4 cups of mixed greens (equal portions of frozen chopped spinach, frozen chopped turnip, and frozen chopped collard greens)
2 yellow onions, medium (cut julienne style – into long thin strips)
1 pinch salt
4 Tbsp. canola oil
1 Tbsp. minced garlic
1 Tbsp. minced ginger root
1 jalapeño pepper (seeded and cut julienne style)

On stovetop, heat medium-sized pan on medium-high heat.

Add the mixed frozen greens and cover the pan. Stir occasionally.

After 7 minutes add onion, salt, oil and the minced garlic and minced ginger root (keep stirring occasionally).

Turn the heat down to low and cook the greens for 5 more minutes.

Add the jalapeño pepper and remove from heat.

Enjoying a traditional Ethiopian dinner

Now that you've made your Ethiopian meal, you have an opportunity to do more than just enjoy good food. A traditional Ethiopian dinner is a social occasion with its own etiquette.

Of course, you can feel free to eat any way you wish in your own home. But if you've gone to the effort to make an Ethiopian meal and everyone in the family grabs TV trays and heads to the den to watch "Wheel of Fortune," you're missing out on a big part of the experience. Here's what happens at mealtime in a traditional Ethiopian home:

Upon entering the home, guests greet the hostess (and often vice-versa) by bowing graciously from the waist and saying, "Selam, tenayistilign." This is Amharic for "Peace, and good health to you." A respectful guest will dress well for the occasion.

When greeting one another, Ethiopians shake hands and kiss each others' cheeks, facing each other and taking turns kissing on each cheek: one … two … three … four. Women greet women, men greet men, and women and men greet each other in this way. Young people are expected to stand

47

when an elder enters the room. Greetings are not to be rushed; instead, it is customary to ask about one's family, health, and job.

Before sitting down to eat, it is very important to wash your hands. (You'll see why in a moment!) Traditionally someone will bring a jug of clean water, along with a bucket to receive the dirty water, and pass it around to let people wash their hands.

A blessing is given before the meal, whatever a family's faith tradition.

Eating is a communal experience. Traditionally, a large piece of injera (20" wide or larger) is placed in the middle of the table on a mosob (basket). Everyone reaches out and tears off the part of the injera closest to them, and the various stews and sauces are placed on top. Everyone eats together from this single, open injera. The hostess adds more pieces of injera and sauces as needed. There are no knives, forks, or spoons at this table!

Traditionally, Ethiopians ate only with the right hand, but today it is acceptable to eat with whichever hand is dominant. However,

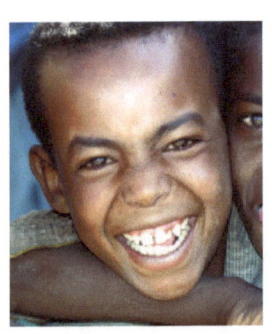

don't use either hand to reach across the communal plate to the other side – this is considered rude. (And you shouldn't have to, as the hostess will be sure to keep you well-supplied as you eat.)

No napkins are used. If you must clean your hands, don't lick your fingers – this appears distasteful. Instead, your hostess will come around with a jug of water and soap.

It's disrespectful to get up and leave the table during the meal. This is true even if you have had to improvise and use separate plates.

Your hostess will bring you more injera as you finish your servings.

In the United States, you're told to finish everything on your plate. But in Ethiopia, that shows the cook that she didn't prepare enough food to satisfy you. She'll think you're not full yet and will add even more food to your plate. So leave a little food behind; this will show the cook that you are full.

When you are finished with your meal, you can clean your hands with water. There is no need to offer to help clean up; your hostess will take care of this.

After dinner, it's time for coffee. If a coffee ceremony is part of your dinner experience, do not refuse – being part of a coffee ceremony is considered an honor.

When it's time to leave, thank your hostess and again say, "Selam, tenayistilign."

ABOUT CLINIC AT A TIME INC.

Thank you for purchasing this book. What you hold in your hand is more than a cookbook; it is providing hope for thousands of men, women and children in Ethiopia.

Proceeds from the sale of "You Can Make Injera" go to Clinic at a Time, a 501(c)(3) not-for-profit organization dedicated to improving health in Ethiopia by reaching one clinic at a time.

CAAT was founded in March 2007 in Madison, Wisconsin by Mulusew Yayehyirad, executive director, with her husband and co-founder, Muluken Tilahun. Their goal was to help the poor and the underprivileged communities in the Province of Gojjam, located in northwestern Ethiopia.

The organization's goals include collecting and providing medical supplies; helping to improve existing public health care facilities; helping to build new facilities; and providing health care-related information and education to health care workers and the community.

Projects CAAT's taken on include the building of a waiting area for a clinic, and the purchase of an autoclave and an electric generator.

Mulusew was born and raised in the Gojjam Region of Ethiopia. "I saw many people dying, suffering – physically and mentally disabled because of lack of basic medical care," says Mulusew. "When I was a child playing with my friends, I used to pretend I was a nurse and tried to help patients by giving them medications and talking to them."

Mulusew fulfilled her dream. After moving to the United States with her husband, Mulusew went to college and became a registered nurse. But Mulusew had another dream: helping the people at home in Ethiopia. "(Fewer) than 3,000 doctors serve more than 75 million people" in Ethiopia, she says. "The infant mortality rate is 100/1,000 live births, and the life expectancy is less than 50 years old."

Mulusew created a unique organization, working from her home with no paid staff, so that 100 percent of donations would go toward improving health conditions in the area.

Because of her lifelong ties to the community CAAT is serving, Mulusew can work directly with regional government authorities, civic organizations and community volunteers there. A committee of trusted and well-respected elders and experienced professionals in the area has been organized in Bichena to oversee the project's execution closely. Here in the United States, CAAT has a board of directors with members representing a variety of backgrounds.

For more information about Clinic at a Time Inc., or to donate, go to www.clinicatatime.org; call (608) 239-3091; e-mail mulu@clinicatatime.org; or write the organization at PO Box 14457, Madison, WI 53708. Thank you for your support!

John-Brian Paprock, original (cooking) photography – John-Brian is a writer, artist, and photographer. He is Priest-Vicar of Holy Transfiguration Orthodox Church, which serves many Ethiopian families in the Madison, Wisconsin area, and is on the board of directors of Clinic at a Time Inc.

Teresa Peneguy Paprock, content, editing and design – Teresa is specialty publications editor at Capital Newspapers, publisher of the Wisconsin State Journal. She also provides freelance writing, editing and marketing through her home-based business, *words & stuff*. She is on the board of directors of Clinic at a Time Inc.

ACKNOWLEDGEMENTS

Clinic at a Time Inc. would like to thank the following individuals and organizations that made this project possible.

Book committee: Mulusew Yayehyirad, Meghan Walsh, Laura Bah, Maribeth Brunsell, Atsede M. (Emuye) Asfaw, Kathi Koppa, John-Brian Paprock, Teresa Peneguy Paprock

Additional photography: Mike Heath | Magnus Creative (pages 11, 46, 50); Niall Crotty (pages 9, 10, 16, 52); Phil Rowley (pages 10, 12, 51, 53, 54); Mark Rutter (page 11)

Lighting equipment: Manderfield Video Productions LLC

Cooking models: Mulusew Yayehyirad, Laura Bah, Mesi Muluken

Miscellaneous: Muluken E. Tilahun, Natty Nation, Christopher River-Paprock, Holy Transfiguration Orthodox Church, Advertisers Press Inc., Rindge School of Technical Arts Ethiopian Club, The Teff Company

Selam, tenayistilign!

www.ingramcontent.com/pod-product-compliance
Lightning Source LLC
Chambersburg PA
CBHW040015240426
43664CB00036B/10